Jews /America /A Representation

PHOTOGRAPHS BY FRÉDÉRIC BRENNER

With an essay by Simon Schama

Harry N. Abrams, Inc., Publishers

acknowledgments

During a two-year period I visited thirty-two states, criss-crossing America from New York to Los Angeles, from the Bering Strait to the Mississippi Delta. I lent a willing ear to every voice, and tried to understand the spectrum of expressions of the Jewish people and of Judaism in America. It was only at the end of a long period of immersion, made up of meetings, dialogues, interrogations, debates, and confrontations, that the execution of this portrait became possible.

My heartfelt thanks go to all of my caring and devoted interlocutors, who nourished, stimulated, and questioned my intuitions. Each one, with his or her respective skills, has enabled me to reformulate this essay ever more precisely. Each, finally, assisted in the birth of this portrait, conceived as a fresco whose contours I sketched, and whose details I filled in stage by stage.

How can I pay homage to a truly extraordinary number of people, to all those who have been the invisible links in a long chain, every one indispensable in the planning and execution of this portrait, without whom it would never have achieved completion? How can I thank all those I never ceased to call upon, and who contributed without measure? How can I be sure to remember everyone, and to find the proper words for specific contributions, which, even when modest, were of decisive importance?

I wish to express here my profound appreciation to all these friends for enabling me to live this extraordinary adventure. For, although the initiative was mine, it became a collective endeavor, in which each participant's contribution played an essential part, as special as it was unique.

Warmest thanks are extended to all those who never ceased to nourish and stimulate my intuition through debate and permanent confrontation:

Linda Caigan • Rachel Cowan • Margy Davis • Karl Katz • Eugenio Masciari • Elaine Matczak • Stan Neuman • Andrea Simon

My gratitude also goes out to those who assisted me in better discovering the multiple representations of a rich and complex terrain:

Bruce Barett • Tzvi Blanchard • Jacquotte and Jacques Bobroff • Zeev Chafetz • Marcy Cohen • David Elcott • David Finn • Jane and Andy Grovman • Judith Halevy • Schorsch Ismar • Jack Kugelmass • Carol and Gershon Kekst • Bobby Malon • Bonnie Maslin and Yehouda Nir • Ernie Michel • Jacob and Joe Milgrom • Peggy and Ted Myers • Jonathan Omerman • Ouri Ram • Eileen Rosenzweig • Nan Ruben • Ellen Umanski • James Young • Sheike Weinberg

Appreciation goes equally to all the institutions, actors, and witnesses of this America, and most particularly to those who by their inestimable contribution at the heart of the terrain will remain the true architects of my photographic essay:

Sharon Abbadi • Dan Adler • The Aryeh family • Rhonda Barad • Tim Boxer • Robert Clary • Harriet Colan • Ron Cucas • Dean and Deluca • Ellis Island Foundation • Rabbi Fein • Albert Fisher • Rabbi Loring Frank • Eva Georgsson • Christine Goff • Danny Goldberg • The Goldman family • Perry Green • Reuben Greenberg • Rabbi Yossef Greenberg • Brian and Myra Greenspun • Michelle Guttentag • Macy Hart • Steve Heyman • Yitzhak and Shonna Husbands-Hankin • The Hyman family • Marvin Josephson • Rea Jacobs • Milton Jacovi • Deb Jensen • Rabbi Lewis Lederman • Marvin Leibowitz • Dr Anne Lerner • Joy Levitt and Lee Friedlander • Tamar Lubin • Jack Mac Clary • Margie McDonald • Nancy Marks • Karen Mittelman • Caleb Negron • Paul and Avi Noble • Mike O'Callaghan • The Ohebshalom family • Harriet Oppenheim • George Parker • Lydia Primisser • Ralph Pucci • David Rabinowitz • Elena and Alex Rosenthal • Sam Salkin • Wayne Schille • Brian and Tammie Schnitzer • Peter Schweitzer • Eric Speth • Julius Spiegel • Wayne Steinman • Rabbi Tuvia Teldon • Troter Antiques • Mary Vasello • Gail Weisberg • Jerry Wetland • Anna Winand • Martha Wohl • All Peoples Synagogue, Miami Beach • Bedford Hills Correctional Facility • The Billings Gazette • Carol Lab, Inc., NYC • Central Synagogue, NYC • The City of Billings, MT • Dean & Deluca, NYC • Dirraffaele Glenn Studio, Inc., NYC • Foto Care – Jeff Hirsch • The Grace Building, NYC • Graco, Inc. • The Hebrew Academy, Las Vegas • Im-Tech, NYC • J.C.C., Comack, NY • The Jewish Theological Seminary, NYC • Knesset Israel Congregation, Miami Beach • Lubavitch Movement • The Luxor Hotel, Las Vegas • Mamiya America Corporation Mattress Discounters • Mayor's Office, City of Miami Beach • The Miller Theater, Columbia University, NYC • Modernage, NYC • Nice Jewish Boys Moving Company, Palm Beach • Parks and Recreation Department of New York City • Police and Fire Department, Charleston, SC • Psychoanalytic Society, NYC • Township of Montclair, NJ • The Wiesenthal Center, Los Angeles • Peg Zitko

Thank you to the organizations and individuals who had the courage to demonstrate through action the generosity of their intuition:

American Jewish Joint Distribution Committee • Best Western, Page, AZ • Best Western Ponderosa Inn, Billings, MT • Beth Hatefutsoth • Andy and Charles Bronfman • Chevrolet • The Concord Hotel: Mr. and Mrs. George Parker • Nathan Cummings Foundation: Charles Halpern and Rachel Cowan • G.P.S.: Daniel Abittan • Mrs and Mr Grodnik • Holiday Inn, Cayenta • Hudson Scenic Studio, New York • Inlet Tower, Anchorage, AK • Kodak: Kathleen Moran, Dick Pignataro, Guy Bourreau, Patrick Gérôme • Myra Kraft • Memoire et Histoire • Mountain Electric, Billings, MT • Pictorial Service: Pierre and Edie Gassmann • The Righteous Person Foundation: Steven Spielberg, Margery Tabankin and Rachel Levin • Rite Lite, Inc., New York • Ronald S. Lauder Foundation • Sinar Bron, Inc.: Michael Mayer • Robert A. Wolfson

At least, an individual word to the very particular people who, each in his or her own special way, through a rare capacity to take time to listen, helped me give birth to this American portrait:

Dan Aiksnoras and Philippe Paul, designers, artists and friends, for all their brilliant ideas • Paul Aouizrat, for his unshakable faith and staunch financial support, thanks to which this project has come to fruition • Adrianne and Mike Bank, my West Coast coordinators, whose spectrum of contributions has been as rich and diverse as their generosity and exceptional devotion to my project • Rabbi Gilles Bernheim, whose moral teaching lights my way • David Friend, for his unconditional support • Ralph Goldman, who believed in my project from the start, and never failed to translate his faith into action • Barbara Kirshenblatt Gimblett, who through her ability to instantly seize the essential, was able to stimulate, nourish, and channel my intuition. In the end, it was she over many weeks who brought this portrait to birth. And it was her well-meaning thoroughness which obliged me to continuously reformulate in the quest for perfection. I pay tribute to her irreplaceable contribution • Michael Levine, my agent, who said I would never sign a contract. Hello, Michael! And thank you • Georges Lévitte, friend, witness, and guide • Egon Mayer, who gave me so much "depth of field" • Robert and Joan Olden, who gave me a home far from home • Jason Ressler, for his persistence in making me reconsider certain "issues". His presence at my side at crucial moments in the long struggle was precious beyond expression • Jeffrey Shandler, whose quality of reflection and highly developed visual sense are allied to a sure knowledge of the terrain. Over two years, he participated actively in the formulation of this photographic essay, helping me find the words necessary to the expression of the ultimate form • Nancy Sureck, whose determination and effort enabled me to assemble the "icons" • Burt Sun, a wonderful creative consultant whose talent has enriched this photographic essay • Jonathan Torgovnik, photography and production assistant, for his exceptional technical mastery and the rare dedication he showed, going well beyond his original role. A true companion of the road, he shared daily the reality of this production, providing me with unconditional support and moral comfort during the most difficult hours • Elior and Téhila, my daughters. May they pardon my too long absences • Myriam, my wife, my muse, my faithful collaborator, for her infinite patience and active presence at every stage of this project.

*i*t's the future. There are no names; just social security numbers. Two men scan each other at a cocktail party.

"Hi, good to meet you. I'm 5487120."

"Hi yourself. 34100987. The pleasure's mine."

"Funny, you don't look Jewish."

So who does look Jewish, Frédéric Brenner wants to know? His entire career has been spent resisting visual stereotype, denying the possibility of self-evidently Jewish appearance and manner. Yet the premise of his work is that there is indeed a distinctive Jewish culture that can be caught in his photographs. Distinctiveness, though, he also wants to say, may not be equated with exclusiveness, with cultural separation. It's the impurity of Jewish life, the ragged edge that frays into the surrounding culture, that engages his acutely intelligent attention. And from the ambiguous, shifting border between the Jewish and the Gentile world Brenner makes his visual reports in startling, beautiful images.

Brenner's chosen work site—on the nervous frontier of identity—is especially courageous, given the booby-traps awaiting any self-appointed codifier of Jewish types. The perilous nature of the enterprise is exemplified by the cautionary case of Rembrandt's "Jews." All that is actually known of Rembrandt's relationship with Amsterdam's Jewish community is that for some years he lived on the Jodenbreestraat and was a neighbor of the great scholar and translator Menasseh ben Israel, for whom he made four etchings for the rabbi's Kabbalist treatise, the *Piedra Gloriosa*. But while attempts have been made to identify various sitters as the true Menasseh, none of those identifications rest on securely documented ground. Of all his purportedly Jewish sitters, only the identity of the physician Ephraim Bonus, painted and etched by Rembrandt, is indisputable. For many generations, though, a sentimental tradition of Rembrandtian philosemitism assumed any figures with swarthy complexions, prominent noses, patriarchal whiskers, or skullcaps to be the painter's favorite Hebrews. But Christians wore skullcaps; old men of every confession sported beards, and olive-skinned orientals could as easily have been Dalmatians, Iberians, Italians, or even Turks as Jews. The face that makers of the "Jewish Rembrandt" legend searched for was the one that had already been sketched by the Romantic imagination: brows creased by spiritual interrogation; deep-set eyes lit by redemptive devotion; a puff-ball corona of holy hair.

None of this, though, was the Jews' doing. The stereotyped physiognomy of the Good Jew, a Prophet shuffling through the streets of Rhineland Gomorrahs, was more welcome, but no less falsified, than the obscenely fabricated phiz of the *Ewige Jude* (archetypal Jew) with his hooked proboscis and blubbery lips. Ironically, the Jewish aversion to portraiture (in excessive deference to the Biblical prohibition on "idolatry" or "graven images") and the equally powerful truism that Judaism was, above all, a religion of the Word, not just distinct from, but actively opposed to, cults of the Image, meant that depictions of the Jews were, for centuries, the creation of their often paranoid Gentile observers. A stock feature of anti-Semitic neurosis has been the fear of Jewish pseudo-normality, cynically adopted to disarm hostility and for smoother insinuation into the body of the host-culture; even, heaven forbid, into its bloodstream. To prevent this contamination, vigilant Gentiles were issued instructions on type-recognition, the better to spot the alien presence through the disguise of apparent ordinariness. And on a less sinister level, the wary Gentile fascination with the Hebrew beneath the frock-coat and spats has meant that we have many more portraits of half-Jews, quasi-Jews, and ex-Jews—the Derondas, the Disraelis and the Dreyfuses—than of Jews. We are familiar with the look of Felix, not Moses, Mendelssohn. Conversely, it was only with the conscious creation of an ethnic counter-type—the Zionist hero—that an inspirational iconography could be fashioned from the stormy brows of Theodor Herzl, the philosophical cranium of Chaim Weizmann, the leonine tufts of David Ben Gurion, and the armor-plated, nicotine-scented bosom of Golda Meir. Doubtless there are images of the makers of modern Hebrew culture—of Bialik and Ben Yehuda—but their essential features are transmitted in texts, not countenances.

Not surprisingly then, it was the contrast between the Old Jew and the New; the *shtetl* and the kibbutz; the *yeshiva bokher* (yeshiva boy) and the *halutz* (Zionist pioneer); which framed the photo-iconography of the Jewish world between the two World Wars. Of course we can hardly help projecting on to the documentary work of Roman Vishniac and other photographers of the Polish and Russian Diaspora, elegiac qualities of which they could never have been fully prescient. But even if these photographs are not self-consciously prophetic, they were certainly conceived to emphasize the differences between the *shtetl* (the world of the past) and the city (the hope of the future); between the goat-carts, the rutted tracks, and timber shuls of the beleaguered village, and the unapologetic robustness of the Yiddish theater; the Zionist newspaper and the sturdy orange-groves of the guarded settlement. Try as we may to look at the images of the *shtetl*, or the great seminar-worlds of Vilna and Kovno, without an anachronistic sense of tragic destiny, the enormity of their fate overwhelms the requirements of historical objectivity, so that it becomes impossible to look at those pictures as anything but photographs that helplessly understand their own conversion into documents of absence. It's as if the process of chemical development were constantly in danger of going into reverse; images emerging from the developing bath refusing to fix themselves on the coated paper, losing their distinctness and substance beneath the red glare of the darkroom lights.

Into this anguished realm of identity-trauma bounds Frédéric Brenner, sweetly unburdened by its desperation and rage. Not that the Holocaust is altogether missing from his work. But he refused to allow perpetual mourning to shadow his lens. His subject is the Jewish sensibility of our own time, so that when, in one of the most shocking images of the book, Brenner invokes the genocide, he addresses himself directly to the *impossibility* of adequate recollection. In the Simon Wiesenthal Center's simulacrum of a gas chamber, a survivor stands, naked, impersonating the fate he avoided. Were this image to have been contrived purely for the purpose of photographic art, it would be an unspeakable obscenity. But, precisely because the video-monitors and the other apparatus of the museum proclaim the inadequacy of communication, the photograph, I believe, turns into an authentically poignant statement about the guilt of survival, the grief of those who have nothing to atone for.

For the most part, Brenner's group portraits are free of lamentation. They are not entirely free, though, of the anxiety of integration which, as Bernard Wasserstein has recently emphasized, may yet pose a more complete threat to the perpetuity of the Jews, than anti-Semitic massacre. But neither is Brenner's work captive to that anxiety. On the contrary, a striking number of images celebrate the cultural promiscuousness that characterizes much of Jewish-American life. Brenner does his best to make "The December Dilemma" (Chanukah Menorah or Christmas Tree?) seem troubling, but his shot looks more like a suburban choice of flavors, and the alternative versions of Solstice light more like relatives than adversaries. Even what appears to be the chilling exception to this soft-focus definition of Jewishness—the startling image of teenage *Kahana Chai* militia cadets—subverts its own hostility by being indistinguishable from any other teenage forest-bonding ritual. The targets, guns, and macho-fist tee-shirts never quite dispel the distinct atmosphere of Camp Matzoball; the optimistically terrorist headgear obstinately remain *shmattes* (carefully laundered by the terrorists' mothers, I bet). In the same way, the Harley-Davidson Bikers, gunning their two-strokes outside a Florida temple, include too many Sharons, glossy and tan—Hell's Yentas in the making—to convey an air of convincing menace.

Frédéric Brenner comes to these brilliant studies of American Jewry after producing similar "representations" of Russian and Italian Jews. But he readily confesses to being infected by a peculiarly American condition: enthusiasm. And unlike his photography in Russia, for example, where Brenner had to struggle to unlock a vestigial remnant, or a stunted bud of Jewishness from the monolith of Soviet culture, in America he has to adjust for the opposite condition: the exuberant parade of ethnicity. Typically, then, it's in the places where that ethnicity is most glaringly colored by the red-white-and-blue—in Las Vegas, Florida, Manhattan—that Frédéric most often plants his tripod, and with results that are by turn joyous, hilarious, absurd, vexing, poignant, and often, as in the case of the Bedford Hills Maximum Security Female Correction Facility Seder, loaded with mordant irony.

Perhaps it's misleading to classify these compositions as photographs at all, if by photography is meant the freeze-framing of a fugitive moment. Brenner has always been more a candid dramaturge, a baroque impresario of cultural encounters. Repudiating the "accidental" nature of photography as disingenuous, Brenner makes no pretense to spontaneity. There are no pseudo-moments of happenstance here; no bogus kisses à la Doisneau. To present his Bokhara and Tashkent Jewish cab-drivers on Coney Island as figures from a trans-Caucasus caravan landed on Brighton Beach, Brenner had first to cover the shooting area with wooden board to prevent the taxis from sinking and then replace the surface sand. Likewise, no one, except Brenner, would have thought of reconstructing an existing *sukkah* on a sky-scraper roof, directly facing the Empire State Building, and his efforts to obtain the necessary building permit turned into a tortured education about the constraints on improvisation in contemporary America. Once in place, though, the chorus line of glamorously dressed, heavily-hairsprayed Broadway stars, smelling of Patou and Partagas, posed between the traditional straw-roof of the *sukkah* and the theatrical gesticulation of the Empire State Building, articulates an entire after-dinner *spiel*, about penthouses and tenthouses, oldhouses and newhouses, wilderness austerity and metropolitan extravagance.

If the intellectually and technically elaborate construction of Brenner's photo-dramas is obviously marked by a French pleasure in the play of ideas, their in-your-face theatricality is well-suited to American grandstanding. Evidently Brenner is moved by the national culture of transparency, its liberation from the inhibitions of European polite taste, and he flaunts New World exuberance with a swagger which, by comparison, makes Max Bialystok look like a shrinking violet. The insatiable American appetite for demonstrative display, the obligation to public utterance, the shameless impulse for turning entire social groups into human bumper-stickers: all this is meat and drink to Brenner's own considerable showmanship. But more often than not, it is showmanship of an instructive kind. Take, for example, Brenner's astonishing re-enactment of a demonstration of solidarity by the sheriff and citizens of Billings, Montana, with a Jewish family whose house had been attacked by anti-Semitic vandals for having the temerity to display a menorah in their window during Chanukah. Brenner shoots the scene from behind the shattered window, recapitulating both the crime and the penitential gesture. But by immobilizing the extraordinary crowd, framed against the half-raised arms of a railway crossing, he manages to suggest the competing sensations of exhilaration and disquiet. What we see is a reverse pogrom: men on horses, robed priests, waitresses, and cops, gathered in friendly resolution. Yet even the ostentatiously multi-cultural nature of the assembly—African Americans, whites, Indians, and Latinos—with their implied embrace of the perennial stranger in their midst, does not quite dispel the air of uncertainty suspended over Main Street. In no other image, not even the "Nice Jewish Boy" Moving Company, where the moving men are almost exclusively black, is the Jewish presence registered more completely in the response of the Gentiles.

Brenner's Gallic alertness to the eloquence of symbols encourages him to scatter them around in his photographs, usually to fruitful effect. The menorah has a particular resonance in the context of the Billings vandalism, because the Chanukah story turns on a narrative of desecration and miraculous purification. Brenner's characteristically generous and expansive variation on the ancient narrative is to emphasize the ethnic heterogeneity of the Montana Maccabees, as if a coalition of Samaritans, Hittites, and Jebusites had been mysteriously summoned to the defence of Jerusalem. Likewise, the eerily disturbing group portrait of the Bedford Hills Jail Seder depends for its power on the relationship between the narrative of the exodus—the heart of the Passover service, with its emphasis on freedom from bondage, and the brutal denial of Exit, signposted at the back of the prison room. The jarring impression that the inmates, with their careful coiffures, might easily be our own sister Rivka or Aunt Esther only maximizes the shock of the paradox. Their next year will certainly *not* be in Jerusalem.

Brenner is best, I think, when observing serendipitous mirror images between Jews and non-Jews. One such image—of Navajo Indians—is literally caught in the wing mirror of a car driving through Monument Valley, Arizona.

Constructing a complicated pattern of inter-related yet discontinuous visual fields and groups worthy of Veláquez at his most demanding, Brenner counterpoints the Indians with a group of Jewish pilgrims, come to the sacred place to read the opening chapters of Genesis on *Shabbat Bereshit*, the day when the year-long reading of the Torah is begun again. There is no facile claim to the interchangeability of faiths here; and the car-mirror that performs the pairing is a deliberate reminder of its contrivance. Yet for all the unbridgeable differences, the primordially ancient desert wilderness (Brenner being as interesting a photographer of landscape as he is of townscape) does somehow manage to wrap the creation cosmologies of the two tribes together, never slighting *either* their alterity or their common humanity. Elsewhere in the book there is a sweet memento of the generations of Levi Strauss, the epitomising union of the Jewish dry-goods peddler with the cowhand. But it's the other Lévi-Strauss who has really set his mark on Brenner's dramatization of the Structuralist Shabbat in Monument Valley.

There are places where Brenner lets his innocent pleasure in what might be called occident-orientalism prompt his comic muse. The carpet that flies mysteriously along a New Jersey suburban street, carrying its load of Iranian-Jewish rug traders, is the kind of surreal disruption of expectations he enjoys indulging; so is the painstakingly assembled pyramid of Hebrew Academy Students (not all of them Jews) posed alongside the pseudo-Egyptian splendors of the Luxor Hotel, Las Vegas.

Equally there are places where Frédéric Brenner takes immense, even foolhardy risks of tone and sensibility, and his most self-consciously startling groups will certainly be found distressing by those who fail to credit the integrity and conviction of his conceptions. It could be objected, for example, that his hauntingly beautiful circle of women, shot in darkness, the daughters' heads resting on the shoulders of their mothers as they seem to perform a danced dirge in space, was already sufficiently emotionally charged, given that the older women were all Holocaust survivors. *Dayenu*, as the Seder song goes, enough already. Why add the gratuitous element that the daughters also happen to be lesbian, as if *their* burden could ever be remotely equivalent to the suffering of their mothers? But Brenner, I think, does not pose a jejune equivalence. What moves him here is the mutuality of love; of *bodily* support, given the one to the other. And he has found a genuinely poetic form in which to make it eloquent; the circularity of the group proclaiming their perpetuation against the odds. It's difficult, in fact, to think of many other contemporary photographers, especially males, who are prepared to treat female experience with such compassionate intensity. It's this corporeal sympathy that permits Brenner to go to places from which most male photographers have forbidden themselves. To describe, verbally, the extraordinary picture of half-naked mastectomy patients is to provoke understandable suspicions of sensationalism. To see it, though, is to have those suspicions immediately confounded in the presence of heroic dignity; the absolute denial of sentimentality; the equally absolute perception of unforced and uncompromised vitality. It is a picture which actually glows with rude health.

Though Brenner's great *tableaux* of Jewish-American life make up the heart of this "Representation," they do not constitute all of it. At the back is a marvelously rich inventory of objects, signs, inscriptions, gathered from the immense diversity of quotidian Jewish life in America (though, at times the images give the impression that Jewish America stops at the Hudson River). The very randomness of the selection makes a welcome counterpoint to the studied orchestration of places and faces that dominate the rest of the book. But often enough they carry the same wry, quizzical look that Brenner brings to all his subjects, his generous merriment at the cultural oxymorons of Jewish America: the kosher cappuccino; the talk-show Mishnah broadcast; Fiorello La Guardia, who could be claimed simultaneously as a son of the Italians and the Jews; the Jericho Dairy Bar and "Howard Stern for Governor" posters.

Between the portrait groups and the inventory, Brenner has assembled what he calls his "Jewish Icons." Few of the chosen subjects will come as a surprise, and it's hard to believe that our sense of Jewish America is much enriched by yet another portrait of Itzhak Perlman or Lauren Bacall, lovely people and great talents though I'm sure they are. And some of the inclusions—Ruth Westheimer for example—are simply ridiculous. In fairness, of course, these are not just celebrity portraits of *gantze machers*, tribal Big Shots. Brenner's framing device is evidently meant to parody the conventional publicity portrait and to ironise both the sitters' sense of themselves and the projection of those images. Thus Saul Bellow's three-quarter profile exaggerates the dandyism of his own self-consciousness and Avedon's frame within a frame makes a similarly unsubtle point. (Let's hope he never gets to return the compliment by photographing Frédéric.) Occasionally, the selective exploitation of framed space works brilliantly to emblematise both the working identity of the sitters and the public persona. Steven Spielberg, for example, is posed with his elbow projecting through the bottom edge of the frame, the black space above him becoming in effect, an unlit frame of film awaiting his creative attention. Ed Koch bursts irrepressibly through his frame with a snap of his suspenders, his thumbs hoisted into the air, filling it completely as if to ensure there was no space left for anything but the public man.

There is unquestionably much to enjoy in this portrait gallery, not least Brenner's expressive way of posing hands. Often enough it's the hands that do the talking more eloquently than the faces: Ralph Lauren's stylish knuckles; Mailer's palms laid flat on the outside of the frame, ready for . . . something; Michael Ovitz's right folded into his left waiting for someone to make his day. And there are, of course, important precedents for attempting to embody the essence of a culture through a portrait gallery of its Talents: the Kit-Kat Club of the late Stuart and Hanoverian Whigs; Felix Nadar's engraved procession of literary lights in mid-nineteenth-century Paris, for example. But Brenner's clear intention to undercut the working assumptions of celebrity photography is itself undercut by the predictability of his choices, very much a selection made from a transatlantic distance. Lacking real sharpness, the satire begins to stick and cloy and develop a bad case of ingratiation.

Amazingly, though, the cliches fall away when Brenner relocates all these portraits to Ellis Island in one of the great *coups de théâtre* of the book (p. 65). Crowded on to a scaffolding against the backdrop of the Manhattan skyline, the celebrities are wonderfully transformed into a jumbled line of immigrants, dressed up for admission, or even more astonishingly into their *baggage*, jumbled together, the piles of faces and hands and torsos rhyming with the blocks and towers projecting into the sky behind them. And we cease to care (or be embarrassed) that Philip Roth has been turned horizontal (in a feeble play on his favorite acrobatics) or that Dustin Hoffman appears to be pointing towards Ireland or that the lovely portrait of Meyer Schapiro for some reason has been turned into a half-submerged pixie. We don't even care that Henry Kissinger appears to be weighing heavily above the folded knees of his nemesis Allen Ginsberg. None of these assorted gestures matter at all beside the crumpling of celebrity into the clamorous array of people who seem to be our relatives, brought together for some mysterious *simcha*—a celebration—on an island at the threshold of Liberty. Crowded together, you don't see FAME; you think instead, oy, watch out for cousin Barbra's nails; and be polite when Uncle Miltie tells you that joke *again*; and did you hear about poor Milkie, and that Isaac with his fiddle, he hasn't aged a day and Ralphie, you just take a look at his shiksas if you should forgive the expression and so, *nu*, what can I say?

Wondrous though this conceit is, it's for his depiction of the unknown, not the known, that Frédéric Brenner deserves to be thought of as one of the great visual chroniclers of Jewish life. For myself (I should be so lucky), I'd gladly trade in the whole Ellis Island gang for the stunningly beautiful and deeply affecting group of the family of Marvin Josephson and Tina Chen in their Upper East Side apartment. Josephson, with his flat, square face, itself oddly reminiscent of the figurines from the ancient Chinese-Jewish community of Kaifeng, is seated at the foot of a staircase on which his wife and daughter stand, while the other daughter, Rebekah Chen-Josephson, is present both directly and in a mirror image, half-turned toward a Sung porcelain horse. In its movement back and forth through sectioned space, it's delicate sense of travel through eastern and western worlds, the photograph is fusion music of the most exquisite and spellbinding kind.

And yes, I know, the Josephsons are not exactly your typical Jews. But then again, nor are the Lubavichers. Nor are any of us, as Frédéric Brenner, thank God, well knows.

2 Singles Weekend in the Catskills, Concord Hotel, Kiamesha Lake, New York, 1994
Total number of participants : 2,684

4   Josephson Family, Upper East Side, New York City, 1994

From left to right :
Marvin Josephson, entrepreneur; YiLing 旖玲 *Livia* לביאה *Chen-Josephson, student;*
Tina Chen, actor/director; YiPei 旖沛 *Rebekah* רבקה *Chen-Josephson, student*

6   Minyan of the Stars, *Sukkah* in the Sky, New York City, 1994

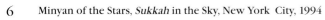

From left to right:
Julie Budd; Mike Burstyn; Tovah Feldshuh; Mickey Freeman; Claire Barry;
Ron Eliran; Marilyn Michaels; Byron Janis; Bess Myerson; Lou Jacobi

8   Jews with Hogs, Miami Beach, Florida, 1994

In alphabetical order:
Brothers Doug and Russell Abott, bail bondsmen; Larry Abrams, police officer; Bill Benesty, owner of custom auto detail shop;
Matt Berkman, liquor store owner; Arnie Blostin, attorney; Chelsea, home inspector; Herb Cohen, magistrate; Jack Davis, real
estate investor; Allen Gold, real estate investor; Linda Holland, medical salesperson; Fred and Amy Krutel, and son Jeff, owners of
a coffee bar; Marvin Lebovitz, general contractor and Harley-Davidson dealer; Caryn Levin, real estate broker; Debbie Marlow,
student; Laura Weiner, accountant; Michael Young, private investigator

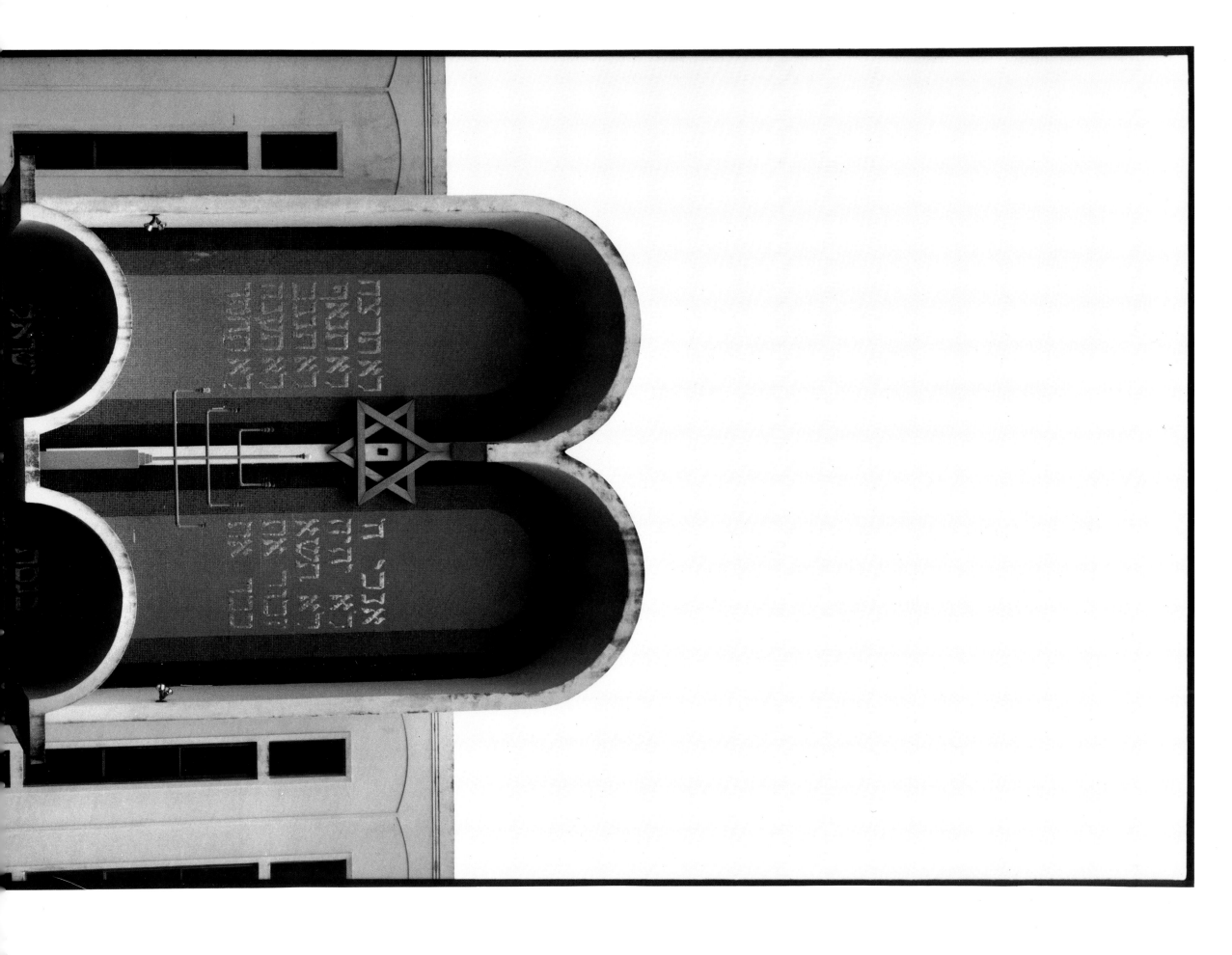

10   Descendants of the Family of Levi Strauss (1829–1902): The Goldman Family, San Francisco, California, 1994

Richard and Rhoda Goldman, with children John, Douglas, and Susan; John and Marcia Goldman, with children Aaron and Jessica; Douglas and Lisa Goldman, with children Jason, Matthew, and Jennifer; Susan and Michael Gelman, with children Samuel, Sarah, and Rachel

12 Gay and Lesbian Families, Desert Room, Brooklyn Botanic Garden Greenhouse, New York, 1994

In alphabetical order :
Andy Mirer, Eliot Pilshaw, and their son, Erez-Louis Mirer ("adopted"); Marjorie Otter, Roberta Steinberg, and their son, Jacob-
Robert Steinberg-Otter ("by anonymous sperm donor; Roberta is the biological mother"); Elizabeth Salen, Jean Lerner, and their
daughter, Ruth Lerner ("the father is known"); Wayne Steinman, Sal Iacullo, and their daughter, Hope Steinman-Iacullo
("adopted"); Hillary Wyler, Carol David, and their son, Andrew Wyler-David ("it's nobody's business")

14   International Jewish Arts Festival, Suffolk Y Jewish Community Center, Commack, Long Island, New York, 1995
"World's largest Jewish performing arts festival"

The Hebrew Academy, The Luxor, Las Vegas, Nevada, 1994

Director Tamar Lubin, born in Mea Shearim, Jerusalem: "This is a community Hebrew day school, which gathers students from all walks of life; fifteen percent of the children are non-Jews. Here we teach ethical monotheism."

18   Kahana Chai Summer Camp, upstate New York, 1994
      Exact location unknown

20 **Perry Green, Fur Trader, Son of David Green (1904–1971) with Inuit, Saint Lawrence Island, Alaska, 1994**

David Green, the son of a furrier, was born in Galicia in the town of Kolodrobka and emigrated to America as a young boy. While still in Europe, he read Jack London novels, and at the age of eighteen left New York for the land of his dreams: Alaska. After many adventures, he reached the town of Ketchikan in 1922. From there he went to Cordova, a mining, fishing, and fur-trading town on Prince William Sound. He traveled throughout Alaska, trading in furs, living his dream of the "call of the wild." Perry Green continues the family tradition of trading in furs. He is also a World Series of Poker participant and has won three World Series of Poker championships.

New York Psychoanalytic Society, New York City, 1994

In alphabetical order:
Harold Blum; Donald Coleman; Sidney Furst; Milton Jacovi; Luba and Richard Kessler; Beatriz and Marc Markman Rubins;
Peter Neubauer; Arlene and Arnold Richards; Barbara R. Rosenfeld; Howard H. Schlossman; Irving Steinschein

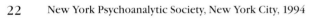

24 Jewish Lesbian Daughters of Holocaust Survivors, with Their Mothers, New York City, 1994

In alphabetical order:
Susan Kan, daughter of Francisca Kan, who survived by hiding with a Christian family in Amsterdam; Nancy Marks, daughter of Lina Marks, who survived by hiding in the south of France on a farm under the supervision of a convent; Frida Neyman, daughter of Paula Neyman, who survived by hiding in the Vilna ghetto, then in many concentration camps, among them Strasshof, Sophienwalde, and Kaiserwald; Lisa Rosenthal, daughter of Kristene Rosenthal Keese, who survived using false papers in the Warsaw ghetto, then in Warsaw and in the outskirts of a village; Sue Weiss, daughter of Athalia Weiss, who survived by hiding in the woods in Poland; Martha Wohl, daughter of Bertha Bauer Wohl, who survived the Rottatyn ghetto, then by hiding in the forest in Ukraine

26   Mothers Who Had Their First Child after the Age of Forty, Dean and Deluca, Soho, New York City, 1994

In alphabetical order:
Shayna Baecker Magid, artist, and her daughter, Elizabeth Sidney Magid; Beth Bronner, AT&T senior executive, and her daughter,
Eva Billie Singer; Susan Farkas, senior producer for NBC Dateline, *and her son, Samuel Isaac Farkas Lieberman; Stella Flame,*
clothing designer, and her daughter, Sabrina Martine Flame Somers; Linda Heller, writer, and her son, Alexander Nathaniel
Lappin; Mary Katz, psychologist, and her daughter, Rachel Katz; Rhonda Kirshner, attorney with Paine Webber, Inc., and her son,
Nicholas Samuel Levine; Marissa Piesman, attorney with the New York State Department of Law, and her daughter, Leah Marks;
Stephanie Rothchild, music business manager for Charles Rothchild Productions, and her daughter, Jesse Ariel Rothchild

Survivors, Los Angeles, California, 1994

From left to right:
Ann Groscher, since January 1982; Sandra Cohen, since September 1990; Dina Metzger, since February 1977; Shirlee Cutler,
since January 1969 and July 1981; Harriet Oppenheim, since July 1976; Susan Branman, since November 1982

30   Spiritual Gathering: Navajos and Jews, Monument Valley, Arizona, 1994

In alphabetical order:
Ephraim Eisen; Rabbi Yaakov Moshe Gabriel; Cindy Gabriel; Rabbi Ayla Grafstein; Rabbi Yitzhak Husbands-Hankin;
Shonna Husbands-Hankin; Judith Hankin ; Steven Klemow; Dorothy Neboyia; Chauncey Neboyia; Rabbi Michael Plotnick;
Ron Proctor; Daniel Staley; Mary Staley

32 Mass Conversion, "All Peoples Synagogue," Rabbi Loring Frank, Miami Beach, Florida, 1994

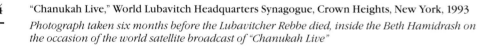

34   "Chanukah Live," World Lubavitch Headquarters Synagogue, Crown Heights, New York, 1993
*Photograph taken six months before the Lubavitcher Rebbe died, inside the Beth Hamidrash on
the occasion of the world satellite broadcast of "Chanukah Live"*

Faculty, Students, Rabbis, and Cantors, Jewish Theological Seminary of America, New York City, 1994

From left to right:
Rachel Aranoff, rabbinical student, Jewish Theological Seminary; Jill Jacobs, student, Columbia College; Caitlin Bromberg, student, Cantors Institute, Jewish Theological Seminary; Tania Caracushansky, rabbinical student, Jewish Theological Seminary; Rachel Lerner, student, Ramaz Upper School; Rabbi Pamela Jay Gottfried; Miriam Gelfand, student, Cantors Institute, Jewish Theological Seminary; Rachel Berger, student, Frisch Yeshiva High School; Dr. Anne Lapidus Lerner, Vice Chancellor, Jewish Theological Seminary; Marcey Bergman, student, Cantors Institute, Jewish Thelogogical Seminary

The December Dilemma, Colan Family, Staten Island, New York, 1993

From left to right:
Andrea, Victoria, Harriet holding Alyssa, Michael, Brian, and Roxy the dog. Harriet is a secretary; Michael is a truck driver.

40 Passover 5754, Maximum Security Women's Correctional Facility, Bedford Hills, New York, 1994
Identities of the inmates withheld

42 Three Brothers' Restaurants, Hyman Family, Charleston, South Carolina, 1993

From left to right:
Aaron Hyman, owner of Aaron's Deli; Phyllis Hyman, mother of Aaron, Eli, and Josh; Eli Hyman, owner of Hyman's Seafood.
Josh Hyman, previous owner of Nosh with Josh, who sold his restaurant to Aaron and Eli upon emigrating to Israel in
December 1993. Aaron and Eli transformed Nosh with Josh into an oyster bar. There is no longer a glatt kosher restaurant in
downtown Charleston.

44   Holocaust Survivors in the Hall of Testimony, the Simon Wiesenthal Center, Beit Hashoah Museum of Tolerance,
      Los Angeles, California, 1994

From left to right:
Vernon Rusheen, 104502: Berlin, Dachau, Muehldorf, Woodland Hills; Si Frumkin, 82191: Kovno, Dachau, Studio City; Louis
Posner, 117657: Berlin, Boulogne-sur-Mer, Auschwitz, Mission Viejo; Robert Clary, A-5714: Paris, Drancy, Ottmuth, Blechhammer,
Gross-Rosen, Buchenwald, Paris, Beverly Hills; Zoltan Friedman, A-12436: Satoraljaujhely, Landwirtschaff, Birkenau, North Hollywood

46 Nice Jewish Boys, Palm Beach, Florida, 1994

In alphabetical order:
Jerry Burnstein; Joacin Cidieo; David Daniels; Jose A. Dossantos; Chris Fierro; Tom Howard; Allen Jason; David Jeter; Bill Lawry; Ulysses Mathis; Torry McIntosh; Sammie McKay; Joe Nunnally; Anthony Rutledge; Donald Singleton; Stacy J. Telfare; Gary Thompson; David Thornton; Earnest Turnipseed; Nathan Walker

48 Reenactors, Battle of Cedar Creek, Virginia (1864), 1994

In alphabetical order:
Marc Adler, Oceanside, NewYork: Captain, Company H, 119th New York Infantry
Richard Bidicoff, West Babylon, New York: Private, 119th New York Infantry
Morton Burger, Brooklyn, NewYork: Sergeant Major, Company H, 119th New York Infantry
Seth Kimmel, Lodi, New Jersey: Private, Company H, 119th New York Infantry
Michael Kraus, Westfield Center, Ohio: Colonel, 116th Pennsylvania Volunteers
Stan Lechner, Northport, New York: Captain, 15th New York Engineers
Phil Levy, Ithaca, New York: Private, Company K, 1st Pennsylvania Reserves
Irving Rider, Erie, Pennsylvania: Private, 83rd Pennsylvania Volunteers
Alan Tischler, Winchester, Virginia: Private, 5th New York Duryea Zouaves

50   Marxists, New York City, 1994

The Aryeh Family, Montclair, New Jersey, 1995

From back to front:
Mahin and Ralph Aryeh, antique dealers (emigrated from Persia 1965); Julia Ohebshalom;
Alfred Ohebshalom, businessman (emigrated from Persia 1973); Daniel Ohebshalom; Shireen
Aryeh-Ohebshalom, mother (emigrated from Persia 1965); Jennifer Ohebshalom

Taxi Drivers, Coney Island, New York, 1994

In alphabetical order:
Dzhura Babayev, photographer, emigrated from Dushanbe in 1993
Samuel Chiger, supermarket manager, emigrated from Odessa in 1973
Boris Davidof, air force pilot, emigrated from Tashkent in 1988
Alexandre Firenshtein, mechanical engineer, emigrated from Dushanbe in 1992
Viacheslav Gadayev, taxi driver, emigrated from Chimkent in 1993
Roman Katanov, watch repairman, emigrated from Tashkent in 1991
Igor Kaziyev, mechanical engineer, emigrated from Tashkent in 1992
Boris Khayms, taxi driver, emigrated from Moscow in 1991
Mikhail Mullakandor, watch repairman, emigrated from Dushanbe in 1993
Yasha Musaev, counterman in delicatessen, emigrated from Dushanbe in 1978
Khaim Palanter, division administrator, emigrated from Belz in 1992
Alex Shabrov, taxi driver, emigrated from Moscow in 1992
Boris Shalomov, musician, emigrated from Tashkent in 1993
Yacub Shaurov, civil engineer, emigrated from Fergana in 1993
Roman Yusupov, truck driver, emigrated from Tashkent in 1993

Nathan Sakarov had since returned to Chimkent; Boris Golodner left for another
city in the United States; the whereabouts of Vyacheslav Oylarov are unknown.

Citizens Protesting Anti-Semitic Acts, Billings, Montana, 1994

The following was printed in the Billings Gazette *on December 11th 1993, along with a drawing of a menorah:*
"On December 2, 1993, someone twisted by hate threw a brick through the window of the home of one of our neighbors: a Jewish
family who chose to celebrate the holiday season by displaying a symbol of faith–a menorah–for all to see. Today, members of
religious faiths throughout Billings are joining together to ask residents to display the menorah as a symbol of something else: our
determination to live together in harmony, and our dedication to the principle of religious liberty embodied in the First Amendment
to the Constitution of the United States of America. We urge all citizens to share in this message by displaying this menorah on a
door or a window from now until Christmas. Let all the world know that the irrational hatred of a few cannot destroy what all of
us in Billings, and in America, have worked together so long to build."

56   Rabbinic Couples, New York City, 1994

From left to right:
Rabbi Richard Rheins, Temple Beth El, Chappaqua, New York, and Rabbi Susan Miller-Rheins, Temple Beth Shalom, Florida,
New York; Rabbi Joy Levitt and Rabbi Lee Friedlander, Reconstructionist Synagogue of the North Shore, Long Island, New York;
Rabbi Susie Heneson Moscowitz, Reconstructionist Synagogue of the North Shore, Long Island, New York, and Rabbi Steven
Moskowitz, 92nd Street YM-YWHA, New York City; Rabbi Beth Singer, Westchester Reform Temple, Scarsdale, New York, and
Rabbi Jonathan Singer, Temple Israel of New Rochelle, New York; Rabbi John Hecht, Temple Chaverim, Plainview, New York,
and Rabbi Beth Klafter, Temple Judea of Manhasset, New York

icons

Milton Berle
Comedian

Phillip Roth
Writer

Edgar M. Bronfman,
Charles R. Bronfman,
Edgar M. Bronfman Jr.
Business and Community Leaders

Carl Sagan
Scientist

George Burns
Comedian

Dr. Jonas Salk
Physician, Scientist

Kirk Douglas
Actor

Richard Serra
Sculptor

Betty Friedan
Feminist Writer

Meyer Schapiro
Art Historian

Walter Annenberg
Philanthropist

Richard Avedon
Photographer

Lauren Bacall
Actress

The Honorable Ruth Bader-Ginsberg
Supreme Court Justice

Saul Bellow
Writer

Norman Mailer
Writer

Michael Milken
Financier

Arthur Miller
Playwright

Michael Ovitz
Businessman

Itzhak Perlman
Violinist

Edward I. Koch, Esq.
Politician

Estée Lauder
Entrepreneur

Ralph Lauren
Designer

Jerry Lewis
Comedian

Roy Lichtenstein
Artist

Arthur Ochs Sulzberger
Newspaper Editor, Publisher

Dr. Ruth Westheimer
Sexologist

Elie Wiesel
Author, Teacher, Nobel Laureate

Billy Wilder
Director

Professor Milton Friedman
Economist

Allen Ginsberg
Poet

Philip Glass
Composer

Dustin Hoffman
Actor

Henry Kissinger
Diplomat

Neil Simon
Playwright

Steven Spielberg
Director, Producer

Mark Spitz
Swimmer

Isaac Stern
Musician

Barbra Streisand
Singer, Actor, Director

Installation, Ellis Island, 1996

inventory
june 1993–september 1995

(arranged alphabetically)

1

2

3

4

5

6

7

8

9

10

11

12

13

14

15

16

17

18

19

20

21

22

23

24

25

26

27

29

30

31

32

33

34

35

  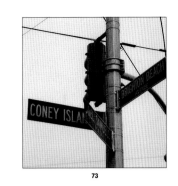    

71 72 73 74 75 76 77

      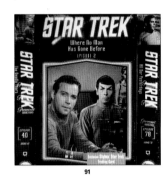

78 79 80 81 82 83 84

     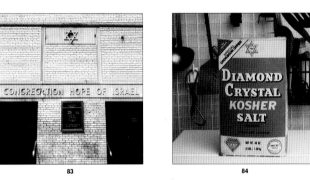

85 86 87 88 89 90 91

92 93 94 95 96 97 98

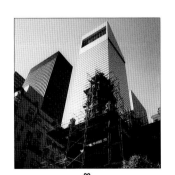      

99 100 101 102 103 104 105

 211
 212
 213
214
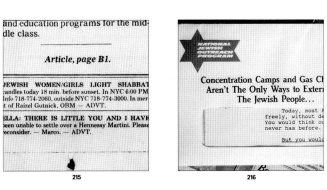 215
216
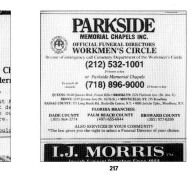 217

 218
 219
 220
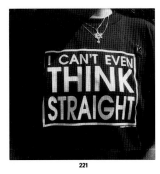 221
 222
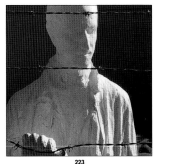 223
 224

 225
 226
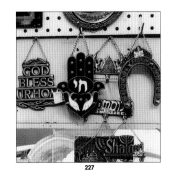 227
 228
 229
 230
 231

 232
 233
 234
 235
 236
 237
 238

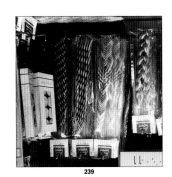 239
 240
 241
 242
 243
 244
 245

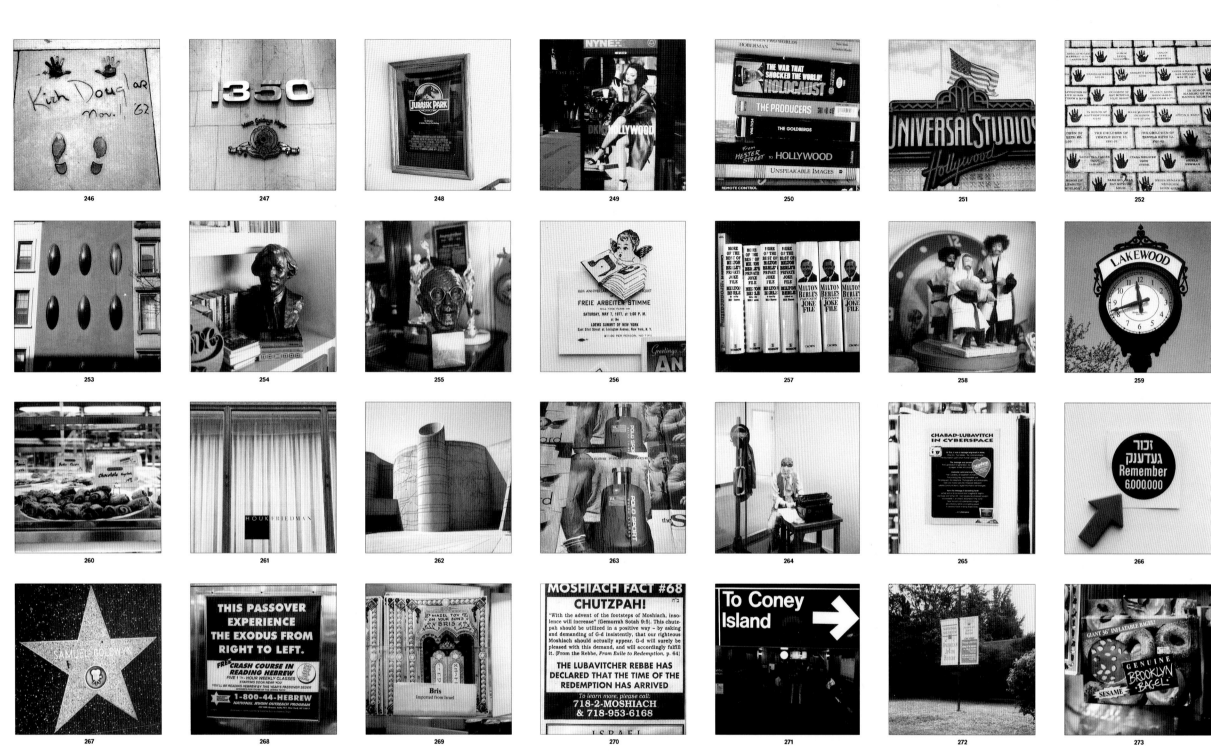

246

247

248

249

250

251

252

253

254

255

256

257

258

259

260

261

262

263

264

265

266

267

268

269

270

271

272

273

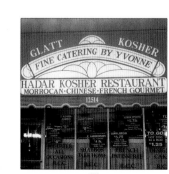

274

275

276

277

278

279

280

351 352 353 354 355 356 357

358 359 360 361 362 363 364

365 366 367 368 369 370 371

79

372 373 374 375 376 377 378

379 380 381 382 383 384 385

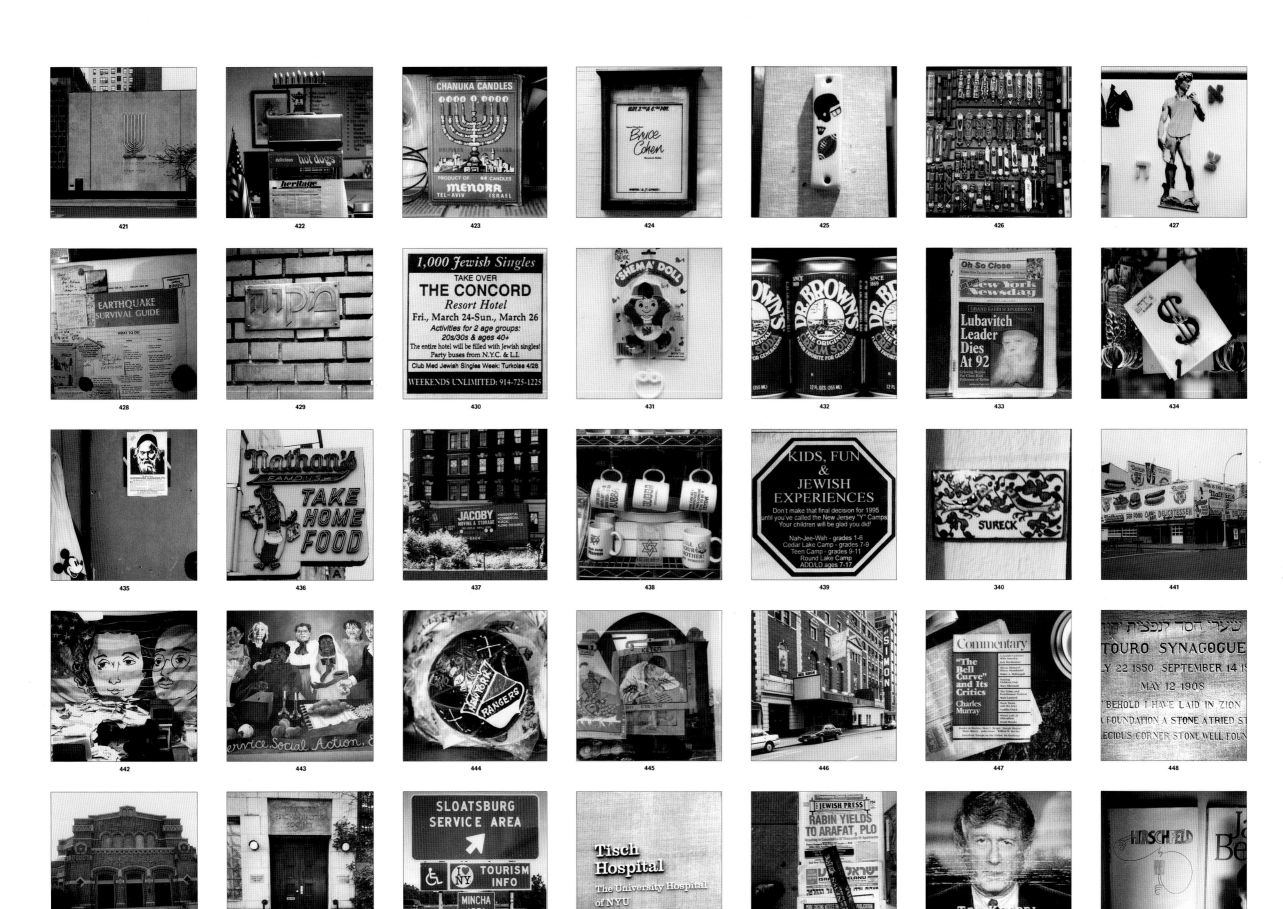

421

422

423

424

425

426

427

428

429

430

431

432

433

434

435

436

437

438

439

340

441

442

443

444

445

446

447

448

449

450

451

452

453

454

455

456

457

458

459

460

461

462

463

464

465

466

467

468

469

470

471

472

473

474

475

476

477

478

479

480

481

482

483

484

485

486

487

488

489

490

 491
 492
 493
 494
 495
 496
 497

 498
 499
 500
 501
 502
 503
 504

 505
 506
 507
 508
 509
 510
 511

 512
 513
 514
 515
 516
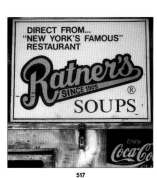 517
 518

 519
 520
 521
 522
 523
 524
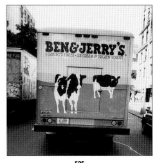 525

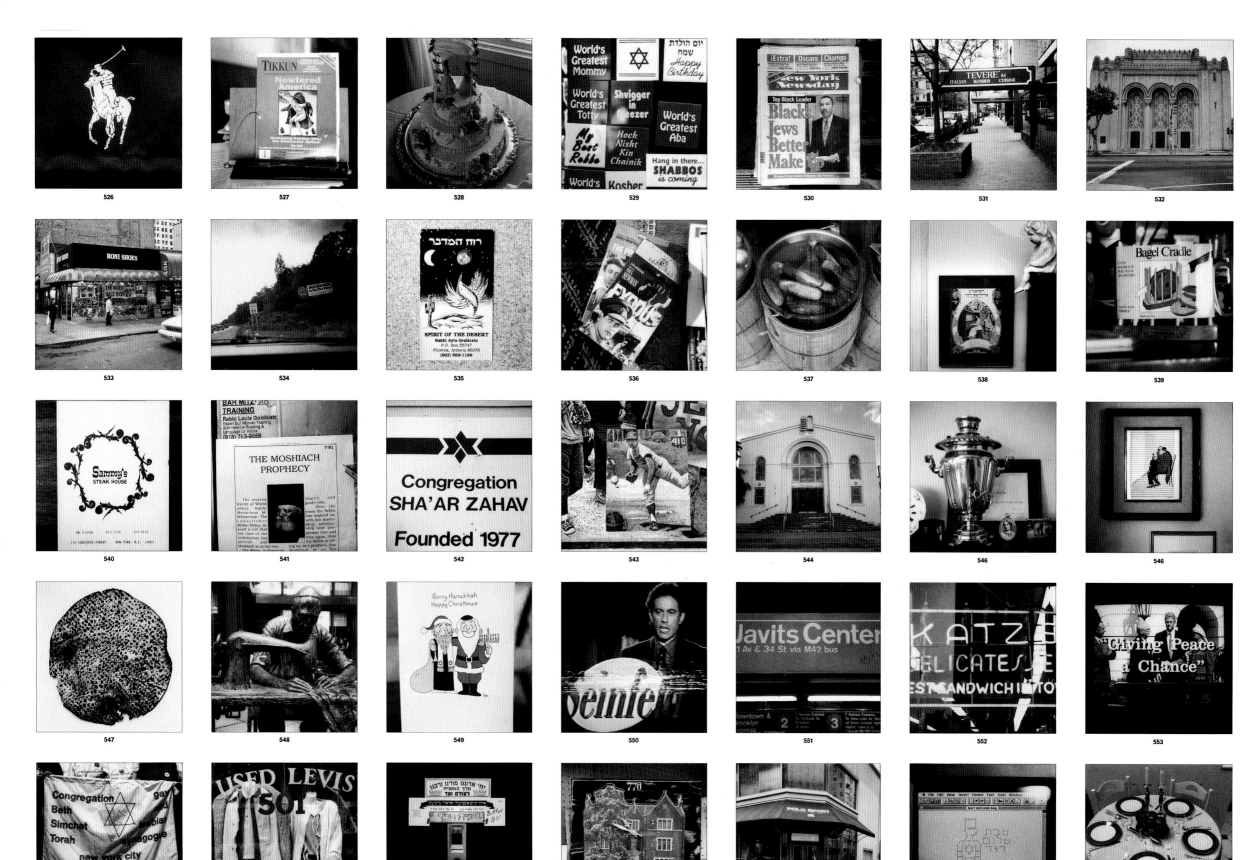

84

561

562

563

564

565

566

567

568

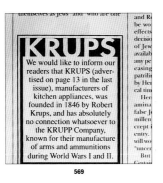

569

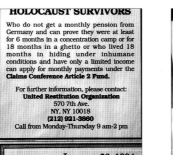

570

571

572

573

574

575

576

577

578

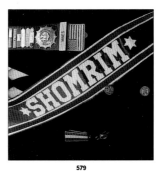

579

580

581

582

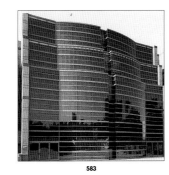

583

584

585

586

587

588

589

590

591

592

593

594

595

631

632

633

634

635

636

637

638

639

640

641

642

643

644

645

646

647

648

649

650

651

652

653

654

655

656

657

658

659

660

661

662

663

664

665

701

702

703

704

705

706

707

708

709

710

711

712

713

714

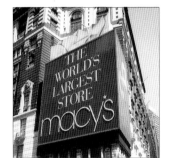

715

716

717

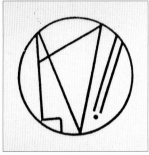

718

719

720

721

722

723

724

725

726

727

728

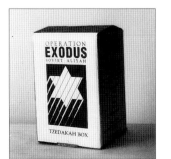

729

730

731

1 "A guide to the direct mail perplexed": A.B. Data 2 "A Heritage of Perfection" 3 Ad campaign offices, Jewish Federation, Los Angeles 4 Adair Kantor, school reunion ID button 5 Adath Geshurun Congregation, built circa 1964, Old York Road, Elkins Park, PA 6 Advertisement 7 Agam (work of art), 530 Park Ave., New York City 8 to 10 AIPAC (American Israel Public Affairs Committee) 11 Aish HaTorah Center, formerly a Mexican restaurant, 9102 West Pico Boulevard, Los Angeles 12 Aisle 4, Food Emporium, Upper East Side, New York City 13 Al Jolson (detail of mural), Fairfax District, Los Angeles 14 All Peoples Synagogue, Miami, FL 15 "All the greatest Yiddish songs" 16 American Israel Public Affairs Committee. Annual Meeting, Sheraton Hotel, Washington D.C., May 8, 1995 17 Antiquarian, New Orleans 18 Arbeter Ring, established 1900 19 Arbeter Ring, established 1900 20 Arnold Rothstein was killed here, November 4, 1928 21 Arthur M. Sackler Gallery, Smithsonian Institution, Washington, D.C. 22 As advertised in the *Jewish Week* 23 At the Polo Shoppes, Boca Raton, FL 24 Atlantic Avenue Subway Station, Brooklyn, NY 25 ATT ad 26 Aunt Sadie 27 Average funeral package, $3500–4000 28 *Avodah Zara*, the first chapter: *Lifne Arhareben* 29 B'nai B'rith Perlman Camp, Starlight, PA 30 Babylonian Talmud, bilingual edition. Art Scroll Series 31 Back to Broadway 32 Bagel and lox, Barney Greengrass, $9.95, New York City 33 Bar Mitzvah boy 34 Barbara Kirshenblatt-Gimblett home 35 Barbra look-alike, Roosevelt Hotel, Hollywood, CA 36 Barney Greengrass, The Sturgeon King, New York City 37 Barney Pressman, founder, 1923, New York City 38 "Baruch Hashem" 39 Beach house of Jerry Stern 40 "Beautiful attorney," personal ad 41 Beit Hashoah, The Simon Wiesenthal Center, Los Angeles 42 Bella Unterberg, founding president of YWHA 43 Benny Goodman, clarinet player 44 Beverly Hills 45 Beverly Hills 46 Blue jeans 47 Boardroom, Joint Distribution Committee (international relief organization), New York City 48 Bobby Schulman, grandfather's *tefilin* 49 Bobby Schulman's living room, Central Park West, New York City 50 Bookmark 51 Born 1902 in Koladreska, Galicia (now western Poland). Store founded 1922 52 Born in France, died in Texas 53 to 69 Boro Park, Brooklyn, NY 70 Brass mortar and pestle 71 Bread sculpture by Shalom Aleichem 72 Brentano's, Century City, Los Angeles 73 to 81 Brighton Beach, Brooklyn, NY 82 Broadway run: 3242 performances 83 Bronx 84 "Build your reputation from cook to chef..." 85 Bus stop, West Los Angeles 86 Buttrey's Supermarket, Jewish section, Missoula, MT 87 Call 212-YSHUA-4-U 88 Camp: co-ed and kosher 89 Canteen, Bardin Brandeis Institute, Summer Camp, Simi Valley, CA 90 Cantor Joseph Malovany 91 Captain Kirk: William Shatner. Mr. Spock: Leonard Nimoy 92 Car service, New York City 93 Cardozo Hotel, Miami Beach, FL 94 Cards for all occasions 95 Catskills synagogue 96 CD: "Music will never be the same again" 97 CD-Rom 98 Central Park, New York City 99 Central Synagogue, 55th and Lexington, New York City. In 1870, 140 families put together $230,000 in cash to build the sanctuary 100 CEO of Disney: Michael Eisner 101 CEO of Toys "Я" Us: Michael Goldstein 102 Chabadmobile (Lubavitcher outreach) 103 Chabad telethon in Los Angeles. Raised in 1994: $3.4 million 104 "Chai," the Lamp of Life 105 to 107 Chanukah 108 Chanukah card game 109 "Chanukah Live" program, Lubavitch headquarters, December 1993 110 Chapter 6: "Never Had It So Good." 111 to 114 Charity 115 "Childbirth," painting by Meyer Rosenblatt 116 Mann's Chinese Theater, Hollywood, CA 117 Chris Christiansen home, Palmer, AK, November 1993 118 *Chupah* 119 City of Peace *talith* 120 Class of 1956, Yeshiva Torah V'das, Jeffrey Ressler's eighth grade class photo, Williamsburg, NY 121 "Classic American" design. About 10,000 sold per year 122 CNN, "Larry King Live" 123 CNN, Times Square 124 Coatroom, yeshiva, Lakewood, NJ 125 Coffee cup 126 Cohn Bros. Inc., dry goods store, Lorman, MS 127 Cold cuts 128 "Collect all 658 Mitzvah Caps to complete your set" 129 Collected works of Elie Weisel 130 Collection, National Museum of Jewish-American History, Philadelphia, PA 131 Commack, Long Island, NY 132 Commandment Keepers Ethiopian Hebrew Congregation, Beth Ha-Tefilah Headquarters, Harlem, NY 133 Commemorative stamp by Al Hirschfeld 134 Computer porn 135 Congregation B'nai Israel, built circa 1900, Butte, MT 136 Congregation B'nai Jeshurun temporary headquarters (corner of 86th and West End Avenue), New York City 137 Converted to Judaism before marrying Arthur Miller 138 Cookbook 139 Cookies 140 Cotton gin, Ben Lemensdorff, owner, Carie, MS 141 to 142 Crown Heights, Brooklyn, NY 143 Davening 144 David Berkowitz, "Son of Sam" 145 Davka software 146 Delicatessen, Upper West Side, New York City 147 Design billboard, Jewish Federation Campaign, Los Angeles 148 Desk of Barbara Kirshenblatt 149 Dial 1-800-AM-I-A-JEW 150 Diocese of Helena, former synagogue, Montana 151 Directed by Michael Curtiz 152 Director's office, Lubavitch headquarters, Los Angeles 153 Disney *yarmulke* 154 Dodgers, Los Angeles 155 E.M.S 156 E-mail Chanukah 157 East Hampton's only synagogue, Long Island, NY 158 Editorial, *Jewish Sentinel* 159 Effusive Chanukah 160 Election, New Orleans 161 Ellis Island ferry landing 162 Entryway, Talmud Torah, Flatbush, NY 163 Essential Judaica 164 Etz Haim Temple, Montgomery, AL. Established 1912 by Jews from Rhodes 165 European marzipan, made in North Bergen, NJ 166 Euthanasia 167 F.A.O. Schwartz, New York City 168 F-Train, last stop before Brooklyn 169 to 182 Fairfax district, Los Angeles 183 Federation campaign, Los Angeles 184 Fifth Avenue, Chanukah, 1994, New York City 185 Fifth Avenue, diamond district, New York City 186 Fifth Avenue, New York City 187 57th and Fifth, New York City 188 57th Street, New York City 189 Fiorello La Guardia, 99th Mayor of New York City 190 First community of Jews in Mississippi, formed prior to the Civil War, Temple B'nai Israel, Natchez, MS 191 Fish all caught in northern lakes by Native Americans under the supervision of the Union of Orthodox Rabbis 192 Fischer Bros. and Leslie, since 1949, 230 West 72nd Street, New York City 193 "Fits all sizes—adult or child; fits all hair types—straight or wild!" 194 546 Fifth Avenue, New York City 195 Flatbush, Brooklyn, NY 196 Flatbush yeshiva, Brooklyn, NY 197 For microwave processor, blender, and crock pot 198 Former Warburg mansion (The Jewish Museum) 199 Former World Zionist Organization headquarters, 515 Park Avenue, New York City, vacated September 1990 200 Formerly Jews' Hospital, New York City 201 49th and Second Avenue (bargain designer underwear) 202 42nd president of the United States 203 *Forward* Building, built in 1912, 175 East Broadway, New York City 204 Founded 1870 205 Founded 1934, Butte, MT 206 Founder of Paramount Pictures. Died at 104 207 Four more tennis courts than Wimbeldon 208 Four works by Saul Steinberg 209 50 East 54th Street, New York City 210 Frank Lloyd Wright synagogue, Elkins Park, PA 211 Frank Meisler 212 Frank Meisler sculpture, Jewish Community Center, Boca Raton, FL 213 From Shmulka Yiddish Dictionary 214 From Telshe Yeshiva, Wickliffe, Ohio 215 Front page, *New York Times*, Friday 216 Fund-raising 217 Funeral director of your choice 218 Funeral home, Brooklyn, NY 219 Funeral of the Lubavitcher rebbe, New York City, 31 Tammuz, 5754 220 Garment district 221 Gay and Lesbian Pride Parade 222 General Assembly, Denver, CO, November 16–19, 1994 223 George Segal sculpture, Holocaust Memorial, San Francisco 224 Gift shop, National Museum of Jewish History 225 "Give me your tired, your poor..." 226 Glendale, CA, "Rabbis Available on Call" ($200–$275) 227 "God Bless Our Home" 228 Golda Meir, garment district, New York City 229 Gossip, *New York Post* 230 Grand Central Terminal, New York City 231 Guggenheim Museum, opened 1959, 111 years after Guggenheim family came to the U.S., New York City 232 "Guilt-free gift" 233 Hamentaschen 234 *Hamsa* (good luck charm) 235 Happy Chanukah 1994, Miami,FL 236 "Happy Chanukah" e-mail message 237 Harlem church 238 Harold Schulweiss, rabbi, largest conservative congregation, San Fernando Valley, Los Angeles 239 Havdalah candles (to signal the end of the Sabbath) 240 Hearsay 241 Hebrew Union College 242 High fiber matzah, not kosher for Passover 243 Hillel Jewish Students Center, Los Angeles 244 *Hineni* ("Here I am"), Jewish outreach organization. Rebbetzin Jungreis on the air. Can be seen nationwide every Sunday at 2:30 pm 245 to 251 Hollywood 252 Holocaust memorial, Jewish Community Center, Boca Raton, FL 253 Home of Arthur Schneir, rabbi 254 Home of Bel Kaufman, Shalom Aleichem's granddaughter 255 Home of George Burns, Beverly Hills, CA 256 Home of Jeffrey Shandler and Stuart Schear, Brooklyn, NY 257 Home of Milton Berle, Los Angeles 258 Home of Peter Schweitzer, New York City 259 Home of the world's largest yeshiva, New Jersey 260 Hot and Crusty *rugelach* 261 Houk Friedman Gallery, Madison Avenue, New York City 262 House of the Book, Bardin Brandeis Institute, Simi Valley, CA 263 Houston Street, New York City 264 Howard Rubinstein Associates, New York City office 265 http://www.chabad org 266 I.D. badge, Warsaw Ghetto Resistance Organization, April 1993 267 "I don't get ulcers, I give ulcers." "An oral contract is not worth the paper it's written on." 268 IRT line, New York City, March 1995 269 Imported greeting cards 270 Increase in *chutzpah* 271 IND trains, New York City 272 Independence Hall, Philadelphia, PA 273 Inflatable bagel! 274 Ingredients: wheat flour and water 275 to 279 Inside the *eruv*, San Fernando Valley, CA 280 Institute for Advanced Learning, yeshiva, Lakewood, NJ 281 Institute for Advanced Study, Princeton, NJ 282 Interfaith wedding, Rabbi Loring Frank, Boca Raton, FL 283 IRT line, March 1995, New York City 284 Isaac Stern home 285 to 296 Israel Day Parade, New York City 297 Jamming 298 January 15, 1959 299 January 1994 300 Jason Ressler's key chain, made in Israel 301 Jazz greats 302 Jerry Stern's 70th birthday, July 1994, West Hampton, NY 303 Jerry's Delicatessen, San Fernando Valley, CA (matzah ball soup, $4.95) 304 Jewish day school. Lower school students, including nursery and kindergarten: 442 305 Jewish Center of East Hampton, Architect: Norman Jaffe. Completely built with natural wood and marble 306 Jewish Community Center, Boca Raton, FL 307 *Jewish Daily Forward*, established 1897 308 Jewish folksingers 309 Jewish mood cube 310 Jewish Museum, Los Angeles, CA 311 Jewish periodicals 312 Jewish rappers 313 Jewish renewal 314 *Jewish Sentinel*, March 1995 315 Jewish "spaghetti" mobsters, directed by Sergio Leone 316 Jewish Theological Seminary, New York City 317 Jigsaw puzzle 318 "Join us! For 72 years we have been open every day." 319 Jonathan Omerman, rabbi, Los Angeles 320 Jonathan Torgovnik home, New York City 321 Juice cartons 322 Kabbalah Center, Los Angeles 323 Karen Mittleman's office, Philadelphia 324 Karina Spiess bedroom, Great Neck, NY 325 Kehiliat Beit Naftali on La Brea, Los Angeles 326 Kew Gardens Synagogue, Adath Yeshurun, Queens, NY 327 Kiamesha glatt kosher 328 Kiddush cup 329 Kinky Friedman ranch, Texas 330 Kitchen supplies, West Side Judaica, New York City 331 Kleinfeld, Brooklyn, NY 332 Kosher sausage clock 333 "Kosher Week," Lubavitch campaign, Key Food supermarket, Brooklyn, NY 334 Lake Como, PA 335 "Land of the Frozen Chosen" 336 Landsberg: site of displaced persons

camp after WWII **337** Largest reform temple west of Mississippi, Los Angeles **338** Learning Annex **339** Learning Annex Catalogue, 1995 **340** Legends of the Jews **341** Leon Hess, owner **342** "Let them eat bagels." **343** Libertarian candidate **344** Library, 770 Eastern Parkway, Crown Heights, NY **345** Library, yeshiva, Lakewood, NJ **346** "Life is short. Play hard." **347** Lincoln Square Synagogue (sometimes called "wink 'n' stare"), New York City, a good place for single people to meet **348** "Look for the union label." **349** Lotz of Seltzer, Inc., Brooklyn, NY **350** Low-fat pareve **351** to **375** Lower East Side, New York City **376** Lubavitch headquarters, Los Angeles **377** M Train, New York City **378** M1 Bus, New York City **379** *Machzor* (High Holidays prayer book) **380** Made in Kiryat Vichnitz, Israel **381** to **382** Made in Taiwan **383** to **401** Magen David **402** Magnetic bagel **403** Magnetic card, Simon Wiesenthal Center, Los Angeles **404** Magnetic *mezuzah* **405** Magnetic seder plate **406** Marvel Comics, owned by Ron Perelman **407** *Mashguiach* (kashruth supervisor) **408** Matchbook **409** Matzah holder **410** Maxwell House Haggadah **411** "May the Lord bless you and keep you" clock **412** *Mechitsa* (separates men from women in Orthodox synagogues) **413** Menashe Kadishman sculpture, West Hampton, Long Island, NY **414** to **423** Menorah **424** Messianic rabbi, Rock Church, Upper East Side, New York City **425** *Mezuzah* **426** *Mezuzot* **427** Michelangelo's *David* with accessories **428** Mike and Adrianne Bank, San Fernando Valley, CA **429** *Mikve*, Upper West Side, New York City **430** "Mingle, mingle, mingle." **431** Mitzvah Toys, Inc. **432** Mom's Bagels, 15 West 45th Street, New York City **433** Monday, June 13, 1994. *New York Newsday* **434** Money clip **435** Morasha summer camp, Lake Como, PA **436** "More than just the best hot dogs." Since 1915 **437** Morningside Heights **438** Mugs **439** Nah-Jee-Wah **440** Nancy Sureck, Apt #2D **441** Nathan's, Coney Island, NY **442** National Committee to Reopen the Rosenberg Case **443** National Council of Jewish Women, Los Angeles **444** National Hockey League *yarmulke* **445** Needlepoint patterns, Boro Park, Brooklyn, NY **446** Neil Simon Theater, Broadway, New York City **447** Neo-conservative organ **448** New Orleans **449** New Orleans, Touro Synogogue, founded 1828. Rabbi David S. Goldstein. Cantor Stephen L. Dubov **450** New York Psychoanalytic Society **451** New York State Thruway, between exits 15 and 16 **452** New York University **453** Newstand, New York City **454** "Night Line," Ted Koppel **455** Nina's father **456** 19 W. 45th Street, New York City **457** 92nd Street, New York City **458** No fat, no cholesterol, no calories **459** Non-dairy kosher cheese **460** Nosh **461** New York premiere, *Schindler's List* **462** New York's richest man **463** New York City mayoral campaign, 1993 **464** O.J. Simpson sermon **465** Objective: companionship **466** Off-Broadway, 1995 **467** Oldest in the United States: Touro Synagogue, Newport, RI **468** 1-800-426-2567 **469** 1-800-BABY BOY **470** 1-800-KADDISH **471** 1384 stores nationwide including Gap Kids **472** 110 East 59th Street, 4th floor, New York City **473** Only Middle-Eastern Byzantine-style house of worship in the state. Oldest standing synagogue in Mississippi, built 1891, Temple Gemiluth Chassed, Port Gibson, MS **474** Original synagogue rebuilt brick by brick in old town, San Diego, CA **475** Oriole Kosher Meat Market, Delray Beach, FL **476** Owned by Jerry Reinsdorf **477** Owned by Satmar Jews **478** Pacific Synagogue, Venice, CA **479** Palmer, Matanuska Borough, AK **480** Parachute Jump and Cyclone, Coney Island, NY **481** Park anywhere, *New York Times*, Saturday, June 3, 1995 **482** Park Avenue Synagogue **483** Part 3 **484** to **487** Passover **488** Passover paper cup **489** Passover set **490** Pastrami and pickles, *Jewish Sentinel*, May 1995 **491** Pastrami King, Queens Blvd., NY **492** "Patronize the kosher butcher displaying this sign." **493** Podiatrist, Queens, NY **494** Pelham Local, IRT subway, New York City **495** "Personal thoughts that will make a difference in your married life" **496** Pewter candlestick holders from Poland **497** Piggy bank **498** Pizza and falafel **499** Plastic dreidel **500** Police officer, New York City **501** Polo shirt detail **502** Port Authority Terminal, New York City **503** Port Gibson, MS **504** Port Gibson Synagogue, Port Gibson, MS **505** Post office, Wall Street area, New York City **506** Power ranger Tallith Kaban **507** "Practice, practice..." **508** Pre-wedding party, Dakota Dunes, South Dakota. Wedding, Congregation Beth Shalom, Sioux City, IA. Reception, Marina Inn, South Sioux City, NE **509** Prepared in Canada for Bubbies of San Francisco **510** "Pretty Faces," Boro Park, Brooklyn, NY **511** Product of Israel **512** Purim party, Jewish Museum, 1994, New York City **513** Purim spoof, March 17, 1995 **514** Pushcart, garment district, New York City **515** to **517** Pushcarts **518** Queens Boulevard, NY **519** Rabbi Moses ben Maimon (1135-1204) **520** Rabbi Norman Listokin, 205 West 40th Street, New York City **521** Rabbi Tarfon says, "The day is short and the task is great." **522** "Rabbi's proud of me" **523** Race Street, Philadelphia **524** Radical Jews, Lower East Side, New York City **525** Rain forest crunch, cherry Garcia, coffee heath bar crunch (Ben and Jerry's full names: Ben Cohen and Jerry Greenfield) **526** Ralph Lauren, Polo **527** Read by President Clinton **528** Rebecca Gorlin and Kim Shaw wedding, Boston, September 18, 1994 **529** Refrigerator magnet **530** Representative Kwesi Mfume, Congressional Black Caucus **531** "Reservation's required" **532** Rodef Shalom Synagogue, second oldest congregation in Philadelphia **533** Roni's Shoes **534** Route 17, NY **535** Ruach Hamidbar Congregation, Phoenix, AZ **536** Running time: 3 hours, 25 minutes **537** Russ and Daughters Appetizers, 179 East Houston, New York City **538** Russia's Freedom Song, by Morris Rosenfeld **539** Safe and simple **540** Sammy's place **541** San Fernando Valley, CA **542** San Francisco's first gay synagogue **543** Sandy Koufax (detail of mural), Los Angeles **544** Sanford L. Ziff Jewish Museum of Florida: Home of MOSAIC (exhibition of Jewish life in Florida). Former Congregation Beth Jacob, Miami Beach, FL **545** Saul Bellow, family heirloom **546** Saul Steinberg drawing, studio of Issac Stern **547** Schmura matzah (Passover matzah) **548** Sculpture, garment district, New York City **549** Season's greetings **550** Seinfeld by Seinfeld **551** Senator Jacob Javits (Republican, New York, served 1952–1982) **552** "Send a salami to your boy in the army." **553** September 13, 1993 **554** 760 members **555** 767 Lexington Avenue, New York City **556** 781 Eastern Parkway, Crown Heights, Brooklyn, NY **557** 770 Eastern Parkway clock, Crown Heights, Brooklyn, NY **558** 72nd and Madison, New York City **559** "Shabbat shalom dude," Bar Mitzvah boy computer art **560** Shabbat table, Olden family, Park Avenue, New York City **561** Shalom Aleichem with granddaughter Bel Kaufman and Tamara Kahana **562** Shalom Finger Nail, 2nd Floor, Lexington Avenue, New York City **563** Shapiro's Sangria **564** Shlomo Carlebach, died October 20, 1994, Heshvan 16, 5755 **565** Shmulka Bernstein's Kosher Chinese (closed down), Essex Street, Lower East Side, New York City **566** to **577** Shoah **578** Shofar with bag **579** Shomrim Society (Jewish policemen's association) **580** "Shouldn't your kids be exposed to more of their Jewish identity than this?" **581** *Shtetl* folk doll **582** Sign of Life **583** Simon Wiesenthal Center, Los Angeles **584** Simpsons *yarmulke* **585** Singles' weekend, Concord Hotel, Kiamesha Lake, NY **586** Smallest reform congregation in the United States with full-time rabbi in 1992, Billings, MT **587** Soho, New York City **588** Soul music **589** Souvenir of Ellis Island **590** Souvenir of Israel **591** Spanish and Portuguese cemetery, Chinatown, New York City **592** Spice box **593** Spring collection 1995 **594** "Star of David motorcycle club" **595** Starring Peter Falk **596** Starring Winona Horowitz (stage name: Ryder) **597** Stephen S. Wise Temple, Los Angeles **598** Steve Wynn, owner **599** Steven and Linda's home, Telluride, CO, March 22, 1995 **600** Steven Spielberg studio, Universal Studios, Century City, Los Angeles **601** Storefront shul, Adath Yeshurun Valley, Sephardic Congregation, Los Angeles **602** *Sukkah* decoration **603** *Sukkot* **604** Sunday, August 29, 1993 **605** Sunday, home of Nancy Sureck, New York City **606** Sunny and Isadore Familian Campus, Los Angeles **607** Sunset Boulevard **608** "Super Sunday" **609** Supermarket, Upper East Side, New York City **610** Sweetened Passover cereal **611** "Swim with dolphins...jeep ride in Golan Heights...gala banquets" **612** to **614** Synagogue **615** T.V. talk show, teen racism, Sally Jesse Raphael show, February 8, 1994 **616** *Tallit Katan* **617** Talmud Torah of Flatbush, doorway, Brooklyn, NY **618** Tasti D-Lite **619** Taxi driver, born 1927 in Sosnowiec, Poland (Holocaust survivor) **620** Temple Beth El, Lexington, MS **621** Temple Emanu-el, 1,500 families. Congregation founded 1850s, San Francisco **622** 10% of all 500 million matzahs made in the U.S. are matzah meal **623** "Tent in the wilderness" **624** "Tevye the Milkman," New York City **625** "Texas Jewboy" (founder of 1960s music group "Kinky Friedman and the Texas Jewboys") **626** Thanksgiving *rugelach*, made with cranberry sauce **627** The biggest piece of property owned by Jews outside the state of Israel, Simi Valley, CA **628** "The complete format for a traditional Shabbos dinner" **629** "The first sound motion picture" **630** The *New York Times*, Metro Section, Friday, June 2, 1995 **631** The only winery in New York City **632** Theater district, New York City **633** "They're history, they're fun, they're America." **634** 13 Essex Street, Lower East Side, New York City **635** Thirtieth floor **636** 3205 Coney Island Ave, Brooklyn, NY, $1100 per person membership dues **637** 1375 Broadway, New York City, two blocks north of Macy's **638** Times Square, New York City **639** Tisch School of the Arts, New York University **640** Tishman legacy, founded by Julius Tishman in 1898 **641** Tools of the trade, Isaac Stern **642** Toothpaste **643** to **658** Torah **659** Tower Records **660** Train, New York City subway **661** Train, New York City subway, Passover, 1995 **662** 223 West Broadway, Missoula, MT **663** Underground rocker **664** Union of Orthodox Rabbis **665** University of Florida, Jewish fraternities, 1994 **666** to **668** Upper East Side, New York City **669** to **681** Upper West Side, New York City **682** *Urim ve Tumim* (worn by High Priest in Bible, Exodus 28:30) **683** VHS cassettes **684** *Village Voice*, April 18, 1995 **685** *Village Voice*, September 5, 1995 **686** Virtual *Shalachmanos* (Purim gifts via Internet) **687** "Waiting for Moshiach," New York City subway **688** Wall of Donors, Jewish Theological Seminary, New York City **689** Waltham, MA **690** Wanted: child **691** Waterproof *tefilin* bag **692** West 104th Street lobby, New York City. Dana and Irvin Kula, Chanukah party, December 1993 **693** to **703** West Side Judaica, New York City **704** Western Wall clock **705** "Where *kashruth* and quality unite" **706** Whizin Summer Institute, 1995 **707** to **710** Williamsburg, Brooklyn, NY **711** "Wine so thick you can cut it with a knife" **712** Woody Allen Sandwich, $12.95 **713** Woody Allen's latest **714** Workmen's Circle Cemetery, Queens, NY **715** World's largest store **716** Written by Wendy Wasserstein **717** *Yarmulke* bins **718** YIVO Institute for Jewish Research, Established 1925, Vilna **719** Yom Hashoah, University of Pennsylvania, 1995 **720** Yonah Schimmel, kasha knishes, $1.35 **721** to **731** Zionism

FRÉDÉRIC BRENNER

Born in 1959, Paris, France

AWARDS

1981 Prix Niepce
1981 Prix du Salon de la Photo
1985 M.A. in social anthropology,
      Ecole Pratique des Hautes
      Etudes, Paris
1992 Prix de Rome

SELECTED SOLO EXHIBITIONS

1981 Galerie 666, Paris
1982 Musée Nicéphore Niepce,
      Chalon-sur-Saône
1983 Consejo Mexicano de
      Photographias, Bellas
      Artes, Mexico
1985 Museum of Jewish Diaspora
      Beth Hatefutsoth, Tel Aviv
1988 Espaces et Toiles Gallery,
      Paris
1990 Rencontres Internationales
      de la Photographie, Arles
1991 Jewish Historical Museum,
      Amsterdam
1991 Galerie Sephiha, Bruxelles
1992 International Center of
      Photography, New York
1993 Musée de l'Elysée, Lausanne
1993 Howard Greenberg Gallery,
      New York
1994 Rencontres Internationales
      de la Photographie, Arles

PUBLICATIONS

1984 "Jérusalem, Instants d'Eternité,"
      Editions Denoël, Paris
1988 "Israël," with text by A. B.
      Yehoshua published by
      Harper and Row, New York,
      and Collins Harvill, London
1992 "Marranes," with a contribu-
      tion by Y. H. Yerushalmi,
      Editions La Différence, Paris

FILMS

1990 "The Last Marranos," based
      on an original idea by
      Frédéric Brenner;
      directed by Frédéric Brenner
      and Stan Neuman; produced
      by Les Films d'Ici, La Sept,
      Canaan Production, Paris

Edited and conceived by Philippe Hessenbruch
Designed by Yellow Graphic, Inc., Paris
Reproduction prints by Pictorial Service, Voya Mitrovic, Paris

For Harry N. Abrams, Inc.:
Editor: Elaine M. Stainton
Design Coordinator: Dana Sloan

Library of Congress Cataloging-in-Publication Data
Brenner, Frédéric, 1959–
    Jews / America / a representation /
    photographs by Frédéric Brenner ;
    with an essay by Simon Schama.
            p.   cm.
    ISBN 0-8109-3522-8 (cloth)
    1. Jews—United States—Pictorial works.
    2. Jews—United States—Social life and customs.
    3. Photography, Artistic.
    I. Schama, Simon. II. Title.
E184.J5B728 1996
973'.04924'00222—dc20   96-12380

Published in 1996 by Harry N. Abrams, Incorporated, New York
A Times Mirror Company

Printed and bound in Japan